THE CHARM CARVER

THE
CHARM
CARVER

DAVID SHUCH

Integrative Arts Press

ISBN: 0-9768136-0-2
ISBN-13: 978-0-9768136-0-6

Library of Congress Control Number: 2005903613

Book production by Tabby House
Printed in the United States of America

Publishers Cataloging in Publication

Shuch, David.

　　The charm carver / David Shuch. — Augusta, NJ :
　　Integrative Arts Press, 2005.

　　p. ; cm.

　　ISBN: 0-9768136-0-2
　　ISBN-13: 978-0-9768136-0-6

　　1. Mental healing. 2. Spiritual healing. 3. Inspiration.
　　4. Peace of mind. I. Title.

RZ400 .S48 2005　　　　　　　　2005903613
615.8/51—dc22　　　　　　　　0507

Integrative Arts Press
11 U.S. Highway 206, Suite 201
Augusta, NJ 07822

FOR MARY

CONTENTS

GAZING IN

Now I sit as the sun goes down and winter calls my name. But I recall the time in my youth that set the tone and the course of my days.

I went to the shore in the mornings. There by the sea, facing east, with my toes gripping the stones, I watched the sky and the clouds take turns with the colors of the dawn.

When I first saw him, the glimmer of his boat seemed a play between the light and my dreams. But then a moment came when I saw the rhythm of his oars and at once I knew what was real.

Simon was old, but his gaze was gently warming and his walk was full of purpose. He told me he was a tradesman, a charm carver from across the sea. He kneeled before me and spoke my name. How he knew it remains to this day a mystery to me.

"Ah, Madeline," he said, "if only every soul had the patience of your gaze, I would not have been called to these shores."

I asked if I might watch him work, for I had not met a charm carver before.

"Come," he said, "and I shall fill you with wonder."

And in the days that followed he filled me with the wonder of his world, and answered questions that rose in me like steam from a simmering pot. And when he had carved his last and rowed back out to sea, my eyes saw then a different world and my soul became filled with new beginnings.

A NEW PATH

At first I was frozen and, in a small voice, I said that I could not learn of his ways. The Elders, I told him, looked on with disdain at those who worked at his kind of trade.

And he weighed me in the palm of his heart, and took me into his silence saying,

"Ah, Madeline!

"A day will come when your voice will sound from centers all your own. And thus will you invite the songs of angels up in heaven. But now your shoulders cloak your heart and your voice is like the shadow of the sun.

"From the day you were born many have paved for you a path—made straight and smooth with polished stones and lit brightly to the horizon. Wishing that no bump would cause you to stumble or drive you to start any question with 'why?'

"And yet beneath their umbrella, have you not wondered at the feel of the rain? Have you not dreamt of the far soaring mountains? Have the stars not called out your name in soft, gentle murmurs that stir in your heart?

"I walk a different path that's paved with rugged stones. It twists and doubles back—down into valleys fogged in with darkness and rising to mountains that touch at the sky. Yet your comforts can not compare to the glories and wonder that I have found here.

"See how your road forks now at your feet! Cross, and many will casually aim to fill up your heart from their pitchers of fear. Comfort and ease sweeten their bellies; even now they lounge. Even now they heap great pity on themselves at the chance that you'll go and choose your own road.

"From here I see the whole of your path—straight as a crystal, smoother than jade. Yet from there you will not even know of my tracks, for they hide themselves from the smallest of lies; they are cloaked by pretending and careless rejection. Only here do footholds come from the strength of your sincerity. Only here is your view brightened just by the glow of your pondering heart.

"My work is not for those with answers, but just for those who hold mystery. If you wish come and walk with me for a while. You'll learn to dance a different dance and learn to sing a different song!"

WORK

I asked him about his work, and he replied,

"Ah, Madeline!

"The world is filled with singing! Great songs
amongst the stars and small choruses in the sand,
and who can explain the difference between them?

"But here are we, between stars and the sand,
singing of our own life and time.

"Listen, my dear, listen. In the tones and the
chorus and the silences, do they not speak along
with the lyrics, but do they truly coincide?

"I listen to the wind. I peer out at twilight. I
sense the life in a thing—in me, a stone, or another.
I hunt for the discordant. I search for the choraler
just out of key and I sit with myself and ask in my
heart, 'Is this for me to reconcile?'

"I have a craft—

It is violent and gentle
It is big and small
It is loud and silent
A shock and a comfort
It is old and yet new.

"People out of harmony with their own private song lose their glow and glimmer and the luster of their shine. Sometimes they need a reminder, something that will stir them in their hidden, private chambers and help them to remember the beauty of their song.

"Then once again they can harmonize with the sand and with the stars."

GATHERING STONES

And we went on a journey to gather up stones. And we walked to a desolate valley where stones of every different kind had come on the flows of a river. Now the valley was dry, but marked by the trace of a once mighty flow.

The path was not smooth but littered with holes—ground into bedrock by currents and sand. Some were small and I overstepped them. Others were broad and I'd fall in, bewildered. Simon helped me out and said, "Your worry is your trap, my dear, gently walk around the rim, but if you peer down you'll surely fall in."

We walked in silence up a steep hill and at once he spied what he was after—a fine crack in the layered wall. Not a crack new to the rock that would have split it top to bottom or crumbled it like broken glass, but an old crack, weathered as was the rock and split along its grain like a pair of lips gently parting. And finding this, he broke our silence.

"Can you hear what speaks through the lips in that rock? Can you hear what lies beneath and beyond? It is a song, younger than these stones, but older than these hills. It sings of ancient summers parching dry an ancient sea and torrents of rain trickling down, deep below ground, finding their way to the hearth down below. It sings of a cauldron, steaming with soup, welling up and up, making its way among the eons, carrying forth across space and through time. And slowly and by degrees this song took on a solid form, breaching this very spot with a lens of frozen light."

And with those words, he chipped away at the little crack in the gray and brown layers. And soon he exposed a crystal, perfectly formed, that caught the light and held it like an ember glowing in the night.

"Ah, wondrous mineral! To you I am less than a wink of your eye; the span of my life too short, even to grow one grain! Now I take you from your mother and put my aim in you. What folly I must be to you! To be worn about the neck of a man for at most a few tens of years, then cherished by a family for at most a few hundred years. In the end it is always the same, you'll be back in the ground, lost, broken or laid in a grave. Away again to slumber for a hundred million years, back in to your mother's womb for yet another genesis. But, wondrous mineral, know if you can in the blink of a blink of a wink of your eye that you have eased the strain within the flash of human life. You shall be held and wondered over, you shall be guarded and possessed, you shall be loved and even hated!

"And if I would change my place with you, I would sing in your place, 'Do not fret with what you'll do, for I shall long endure! To sense your aim will give me more than if I were left alone. Do what you will for it is almost all the same to me and perhaps, just perhaps, I will learn a new song.'"

He became silent and climbed down the hill and handed me this wondrous stone. And I held it tight and it made me so unspeakably glad. And I wondered about this, but feeling so full, I never did ask Simon why.

SHINING EYES

And I asked, "Why have you come?" And he answered, saying,

"Ah, Madeline!

"Oftentimes I see in eyes a wandering. They roam the past and gaze across tomorrow.

Burdened by worries, driven by passions, blinded by a dozen things, deafened by a score of urges—they flit and quiver like a rudderless ship caught and tossed in a violent sea.

"Like slaves to a hundred masters, beaten down, they are dull; without shine. Wandering without searching, trapped without knowing; lost to a sense of their own inner wish, they cast about, shimmerless.

"Eyes without life, life without time; death! But death that walks and stumbles like a puppet pulled by host of strings. Is it better now to live near a hundred years if each moment one is scattered like dust and consumed by what thirsts on one's attention?

"There once lived a clan that built a bridge to those with the secrets of time. And those who crossed returned with the gift of a quiet glow and a shine in their eyes. But the bridge was built of sandstone, and the chasm full of wind. And in their haste, few took time to maintain the crumbling bridge. Soon, it was just a pile of sand at the base of a high mountain pass. Soon the bridge was long forgotten. Soon its cause forgot as well.

"Still there are some who wish to recall. But a wish so faint and fleeting carries no more weight than yet a thousand other things.

"And yet there comes a moment, different than the rest. Giving a glimpse of life with more illumination. And for an instant a bit of time's secret is revealed and for a moment the eyes grow still and glowing. And though the bridge is now no more than sand blown in the wind, in that peculiar moment the chasm's spanned again.

"Word will travel and many will come filled with a thousand wishes. Looking for an easy way to grease the palm of God! But there will be a few who have tasted other moments and come looking for a way to hold a different kind of wish.

"Their eyes sparkle with an echo of a grander kind of light. But it fleets their grasp despite their fervent wish to hold it. I have come to carve a charm for every one of these. A charm to help them cradle this, their precious inner wish. A charm to remind them of a life they sense but yet they can not see. Peculiar, yet familiar; disturbing, yet a comfort; a signpost mute of any help save for its direction. For this I sail to distant shores and will go on to others. It's for the glow, my dear, the shine; the quiet shine that speaks of those from far across the chasm."

AWAKENING

Simon rose early and we would walk the beach before dawn, taking in the quiet sounds before the day began. I'd be groggy when we set off and only awaken after a time. Simon laughed when I'd say that I was finally awake, and when I asked him why he laughed, he answered saying,

"Ah, Madeline!

"The day awakens with the first glimmer of the dawn, and then by degrees grows ever more alive. But who can say just when the day is at last awake? And even in the darkest night in slumber's cradling embrace, are you not awake enough to travel in your dreams?

"I dreamt that we walked barefoot and tossed flattened stones through low breaking waves. Yet did we not just take a walk like that today? Perhaps we are both dreaming now and who is to say what really is true?

"For wakefulness is a rope tossed down to us from heaven. At times I climb using my strength, at other times I hold the rope, resting, and yet ascend as angels pull me from above. But I know not when the pull will come, and in the clouds I am suspended and easily I fall into dreams. Perhaps I am climbing? Perhaps I am pulled from above? Perhaps I am dreaming that they are pulling, but instead they have let the reel go, and I am plummeting down, down, down—but clueless to my coming doom.

"I have resigned myself to this—that in each moment of my life at least a part of me is dreaming. The world will always call me to slumber, yet life continues to stir me to rise."

THE STORM

On a day when a storm was approaching, I followed the road to the outskirts of town. The clouds were still high, but the wind was stiff and easterly. I came upon a gathering throng who had learned of Simon's presence. They formed a line that snaked from the road up to the door of his cottage. And there was Simon, intent with each. To most, he kindly touched their arms, to some he gave a polished stone and, finding relief, each of these stood a bit taller and went about his way.

But every so often he'd meet with one and his eyes would fill with wonder; for this one, he would carve a charm. The two would step inside and then the line would come to a stop. After a time the door would open and Simon would appear. His guest would leave and the line would start to move along again.

This went on till the last of them were scattered by the rain. Shielding myself, I went to the door and loudly called out to him. He opened the door and sat me by a fire. And when I was dry I asked him, "How do you pick which ones you'll carve for?" And he answered, saying,

"Ah, Madeline!

"Can you hear the song of the storm? Now it blows in earnest, betraying any mask of an aimless summer squall—the leaves shrill in the wind, the rain deafens like cannon, and though the sun has yet to crest, the sky is dark and gloomy.

"Not fueled by a casual spirit that's weakened by a passing breeze or faded by a drying heat, this is a storm of substance! Blending wind and water with heat from the sun, here we have a whirlwind. Here we have a spinning flow with force and aim and violence. But a violence that shields a fragile core of peace and light and promise.

"Often am I out at sea and a violent storm finds me. But I have learned the art to find the eye of any storm, and I ride out the bluster in this quiet inner room. There I rest in the light of the sun; there I plot my future course. There to touch the axis of that awesome spinning wheel.

"And though I have been shipwrecked, I count myself a lucky man. For a storm such as this traps many and few find their way through the wind and the rain.

"Lovely and frightful, this tempest reflects an inner plight. Not struggles that puff and blow from trifles—they are like squalls, erupting in heat. But struggles that seize a finer part and steadily blow on inner embers. And driven by their fullness, they circle around an ungraspable core—the eye of their storm; their own inner wish.

"Few sustain an inner storm, fewer yet an inner wish. Days and years are puff and blow and charms cannot affect a squall. But I can hear a tempest wind and see a swirling sea. And if their storm has formed an eye, though they cannot find her, a charm can be the beacon to that peace and to that light. And so my dear, my choosing is this, I listen for the song of the storm—the driving rain and the blowing of wind, circling round a core out of grasp; circling round shy inner wish."

TIME

And I asked him, "How long will you be here?"
And he answered, saying,

"Ah, Madeline!

"What is time but a knotted string of moments? And what ties the knot in this moment we share?

"If I were here as a seagull, perched high above the ocean tide—gazing down for fiddler crabs or minnows in a tidal pool. Then though we were together here I would be away, to the thrill of the hunt in my wings and the taste of a fish in my mouth.

"If I were here with my sorrows, longing for my distant home—recalling those I left behind and the blessed rest of my pillow. Then though we were together here I would be away, to the warm glow of my family and the cozy retreat of my bed.

"If I were here but sleeping, and dreaming of fortune and fame—counting my treasures and floating on a sea of adulation. Then though we were together here I would be away, to the twin seductions of comfort and praise.

"The foolish only measure time in hours, days, and years. Yet it is more that I sense you here, with ears for my words and a heart for my ways than any matter of hours or days. This sacred moment, precious to me—a knot on my own spool of string! Tied tightly and snug by our common attentions, at least for now we are both really here!

"Perhaps I shall sail on the tide tomorrow. Perhaps God's angel will take me tonight. Perhaps your interest in me will wane and though I shall remain, it is you that won't stay. Who, my dear, who can say? In truth, it's not for me to know. All I can say, all I can say is . . .

"I have come with a purpose and, like the mayfly, I sense my breaths are numbered. Yet this is not a cause for tears or celebration. It is only good for this—that I remember and so strive for holiness right now; for every moment holy!

"And years from now when, like the faithful with their beads of prayer, you peer into your heart and finger this knot on your own spool of string, I dare say you won't dwell on things like hours, days or years. But will recall only this—a moment spent together."

ATTRACTION

I remember a day in Simon's shop on a cloudless summer morning; the sun had not yet crested the eaves and cut a bright path through the window. Simon sat by a wide-open drawer. He selected a rock and pondered it, then held it to the light, turning it left and then to the right. He returned it and selected another, and this went on for a very long time.

I took to imitating him and he did not at all interfere. I looked to see what he'd been seeing, but soon I lost myself in staring at the colors. There were the blues of lapis, and the silky greens of jade, and sparkling-brown tiger's eye, and violet amethyst. My favorites were the tourmalines in shades of blue and red and green. I'd hold them sideways in the sun and paint the floor with colored light.

The day before a man inquired for a charm. And I knew that Simon was choosing his stone. In time I grew bored of the tourmaline lights. I looked at Simon, and asked him, "How do you know which stone to choose?" And he answered, saying,

"Ah, Madeline!

"I see your eyes devour stones like wolves upon a sheep! And with a belly full of light, your off to sleep, contented. The play of color stirs your dreams, and now your mind is running. Or else a glitter dazzles you, and now your heart is soaring. Or even your fingers enraptured by smoothness, and now your hands are swimming. And yet if I am so seduced to run or fly or swim, perhaps the stone devours me and I am just a sheep?

"For I have spent a host of years resisting my consumption. And I have lived amongst the stones and toiled at their carving. Their dust is in my sweat and flows within my veins! I know how they carve and polish and how the light goes through them. And even when I close my eyes, the colors and the glow remain, even as I dream.

"But captivated, I am lost; my mind, a dog untethered; my heart, a bird uncaged; my bones, a fish escaping. Divided, I am blind to my necessary task, for I must be transparent, and beckon a stone to track fully through me. Then it is free to leave a trace beyond mere colored light. Then I am free of fancy dreams and idle speculation. Then sitting in its prism, I am not consumed.

"For stones are all attractive! And stones will always capture the eye, yet I must make myself prepared to sense again and again. And not to sense the stone for me but for whom the charm is for.

"And what is attraction but kindredness. And how many ways can one sense the familiar? By situation or desire, by habit or by love, by sounds or thoughts or strivings—its ways are without end.

"I make myself like a bamboo flute, a hollow pipe in tune. And through it I blow the singing of this man. I blow on out his song and sense the undulations, and filled with his music I gaze upon stones and listen then for kindredness again and again and again.

"Then, a moment comes. Holding this song I gaze and at once there is no sense of discord, just harmony and harmony and I know the stone is his. And then the moment passes, and the song fades into silence, and once again I am left with a stone attractive to my eyes, but now, my dear, with a knowing that I did not possess before. And I thank the gentle heavens for this little glimpse of light."

GIVING AND TAKING

One day a squall hit, with sheets of rain and lightning strikes all around us in the sand. And then the sky cleared and two sisters came, the younger, an actress, small but feisty; the older, a mother, tall and gentle. And they kept a fair distance from one another, for when their space closed, they fought in a kind of ritual dance. The actress quickly flashed her temper, the mother slow to show her strength. And when at last they came to blows, the older one subdued her kin, who sprung to overstate her pain. And then, the show over, each stood apart on the still damp sand, the older one again demure, the younger one again supreme.

The actress, still riled by the exchange, made a show of her petition. "Please, dear sir," she began her entreaty, "my sister needs a special charm. For unlike me, her friends are few, and those she has strip bare her cupboards, while she regrets not giving them more."

The mother then looked down and off and in a quiet voice exclaimed, "My sister, not I, is in need

of the charm. For though her speech is full of zest,
she's deaf to any other voice, and though she seems
to look at you, a mirror's all that she can see."

The actress, in payment for her just-wounded
pride, pulled smartly on her sister's hair. The older,
wishing freedom, barely touched her sister's arm,
which brought about horrendous screams. But
Simon dug beneath his feet and found a hollow
tube of sand fused solid by the lightning strike.
And with his hands he broke it in two and tied each
half to a cord of silk. Then handing one to each of
them in a gesture of farewell, he smiled, saying
only, "May heaven help you find your measure."
And they left, bewildered, but shoulder to shoulder.

And I marveled at their change and I
scratched my head in wonder. And after a time I
asked Simon, "How can a tube made out of sand
be a charm to both these sisters?" And he answered
saying,

"Ah, Madeline!

"Who can fathom heaven's power? It's here
and gone in barely a flash, and all we can sense are
the tracks of its trace. First an awesome burst of
light and tears fill my eyes and blind me. But soon
again my eyes clear, only to find a shift in terrain.

"What comes about when heaven's finger touches precious earth? It is always the same, a vessel is made. Yet not like a potter makes out of clay, but more like a flute that sings as it's breathed. Touching sand it makes lightning-rock, a fragile tube with a hollow bore. Touching a womb, it ushers a life, a vessel even more precise.

"But heaven will not be contained as water in a storage pot, for though it knows quiet, it flees from stagnation. And seeking to explore, it flows like the tide. Breathing out, it animates, and breathing in, it hears our song.

"Our greatest tragedy is this, we think that we can hold a lot, yet all we can contain is the music passing through us. And rarely do we pick the tune, and rarer still can we. Yet we can store a kind of strength, and all that strength is good for is wishing for a song. A song with no name, and a tune we won't know until, at last, we've heard it. But storing that strength! It passes right through the holes in our flute!

"The wind of heaven fills me. If I take in too much I'm filled with a fire and glow in my own estimation. But if instead I give out too much, my instrument will never play. In either case I've lost my measure—the gate is yet too tightly closed or yet it is too open.

"Each flute has a pitch, unique—a measure of its length and bore. And splendid music flows when the breath is a match for the measure. A charm is but a wish, confined, but a wish obscured by an unmeasured wind needs not a charm but a glimpse of heaven."

FAME

And I asked him if he ever carved a charm for one famous. And he replied,

"Ah, Madeline!

"Fame is a hungry beast that's filled with an awful wind! And those who pursue it are like fools hunting lions with twigs and a handful of sand. Yet they are not eaten like innocent sheep, leaving nothing but bones; their flesh remains, their countenance brightens. And they become puppets of the hungry beast, insatiable for morsels of praise; always, always grasping for more. Their lives overflow with a striving for notice, yet filled as they are with nothing but wind.

"Purchasing fame and damning its cost, its spirit blows like a violent tempest, leaving just a wisp of smoke at the candle of an inner wish; never to burn, never to warm, never to illuminate the quiet inner corners.

"Yet fame can have a different face. A lion not pursued and with her hunger satisfied grows curious at the lives of men. She watches from afar and they, in turn, respect the beast that gives them each the gift of awe. Fame acquired without pursuit has no need to hear its own voice. It has no yearning to consume and no wind to extinguish a delicate flame. Rather it just gently blows, coaxing the glow brighter and brighter.

"Some blowing with the wind of fame have found their way to my door. I have squinted at the light from their teeth and peered into their twinkling eyes, yet I don't see the flicker of any inner flame. They look to persuade with their words and their manner and promise me riches and offer me fame. They wish for things untouched by charms, but try as I may they don't want to hear. So I tell them they are special and I, a simple man, do not possess the skill to carve a charm for them. I say, "Across the sea in the land to the north there is another carver, but I forgot his name." Receiving this morsel of flattery, they leave feeling full, with their heads held high and a smile wider than before.

"Yet two of the famous came to me with inner flickers of light. One was a woman made famous by fate. She used her fame to shed light on the poor and wished a charm to help her. For her I carved a modest purse of violet amethyst. The second was a man who hunted fame as a youth, and having her cornered, demanded his due. He lived like a god till a terrible plague brought him to the ground. Resigned now to his mortal fate he wished to find a way to be worthy. For him I carved a cocoon out of slate.

"A wild beast is dangerous no matter how magnificent. And how can a candle flame survive in the face of a thousand lights? Fame is like a furnace that bakes a porcelain mask, and charms are a help only when a mask is chipped or cracking. And yet, my dear, I tell you this, the famous do not seek us, for charms are not alluring to the twinkle in their eyes, but trinkets—ah! These are the things that truly satisfy them."

TWO BROTHERS

Once, while I was putting up tea, a pair of men came in, two brothers—a judge, the other an aimless man. And they bickered with each other over trifles large and small. The judge made decisions and closed his mind; his brother clutched at uncertainty like a starving man grasping for a crust of bread, each helpless but to prod his kin to ever more distress.

The judge told Simon, "My brother needs a charm. For his life has come to nothing as he never can decide. Though he lacks neither brain nor brawn, I find him drowning even in puddles; flailing without the slightest effect."

Then his brother spoke, "No, my brother needs the charm. For his life has come to nothing—he won't ever change his mind. And though he lacks neither brain nor brawn, I fear he will die only alone as all who meet with him are driven away by the shiver of his icy ways."

And each disputed the account of the other. But Simon found an agate slab no longer than my thumb, smooth and polished with a hole on each end. And with a hammer, he smashed it in two and threaded each on a cord of silk. Then handing one to each of them in a gesture of farewell, he smiled, saying only, "May the wind of love find a home blowing through you." And then they left, bewildered, but now without dispute; the tea had yet to come to a boil.

And my brow became all fretted with wonder. The brothers, so different, yet Simon gave each a similar stone. And I asked him, "How can the same uncarved stone, charm these two such different men?" And he answered saying,

"Ah, Madeline!

"The wind has died, and I can hear two voices from a mountain stream. Now it flows on polished stones, speaking in a whisper. Then the stream course changes, cascading down a different flank. Now it bellows over boulders.

"Within the mountain, in its core, lies a quiet chamber, warmed as by a primal hearth. And seeping through the streambeds, flow the gravid waters; heavy with their minerals, to spawn another agate ring. First a band of orange-brown, a gift from pebbles far above, next a band of glassy-white, the offspring of a boulder.

"The rings are its seasons, like those of an ancient tree. Yet each of these persists for half a hundred thousand years. A season of whispers, then one of bellows, and on and on through endless time, with each, a trace, distinct, remains.

"Is it not just the same with you and with me, except though our seasons are shorter and fewer? First a voice bellows and then a voice whispers and who am I to choose what to hear?

"Often I am caught in these streams, bearing the pull of their opposite flows. With a strong wish I hold myself still, but if I fail, quickly am I pulled both down and below. Then I am like the jailed man who pretends he is really free and living this dream I cannot tell when the door to my cell is open. Or I become his cell mate, dismissing my crime without remorse and languishing there the rest of my days. In either case it's the same discord—a soul made brittle by a heart that won't ponder.

"And yet I find solace in fair agate's rings, for she pondered the whispers and bellows, and in her heart these, she reconciles. Steadfast, and lacking of hurry, she holds in her core a solidified wish. It's a wish accepting the voices of seasons, allowing each to leave a trace.

"Holding a wish to ponder each voice, my heart grows strong as an agate stone. And yet so few know even this, even if they are brothers! A charm is but a wish, confined, but a wish obscured by a ponderless heart needs not a charm but shattering."

THE FACE OF GOD

I remember a day in summer, a cloudy afternoon. The sun, still high, burned hot on my face when there were breaks in the clouds. Simon sat with a lady who came with a wish for a charm. Here is where he began his craft; to look and sense and listen. Here his search began for the seed that would become her charm. I gazed at him as he watched her. He, like a man parched in his throat, drank of her gestures and drank of her words. As she shifted her frame, he was there. As she spoke in strained tones, he was there. As she paused in her speech and then deeply sighed, he was even more thirstily there.

I once watched my brother pursuing a girl who filled him with a fire. He took her in as a thirsty boy drinks, but Simon's thirst was different. For Simon was not transported; he did not become lost as if in a cloud. And unlike my brother Simon drank, but he did not feast, as his wishes were pure.

I was young, and sat on the ground, near about his feet. I watched to see what it was that he watched, but now and again I became distracted. The breeze sang a song in my ears when Simon and she were silent. The shadows of the passing clouds painted the meadow in swift moving phantoms. And I felt the sun and heard the song and gazed upon the phantoms. And presently, the lady excused herself and left.

And I sat for what seemed a very long time, deep in a puddle of rapture. And pondering the moment, I turned my gaze to Simon, who himself was taking in the day. And I wanted to know what he had gleaned that now prepared him to carve her a charm. And I asked him, "What did you see?" And he answered saying,

"Ah, Madeline!

"I've seen you watch the phantoms as they race across your face. I, too, am drawn to the wonder of veils that gleam between us and the sun. Here I am, tied to life by a golden cord that feeds me from the Great Beyond. Never far from breaking, never far from the time of my return, I stand in the face of a passing shadow, thrilling at my luck. For soon enough the phantom will tarry, and the veils will be like a dark velvet cloak. For now I can remember, the phantoms still race; my golden cord, for now secure.

"I am filled with a wonder of veils; thrilled with how quick they can bring me around. Yet some are more than a cloud or a breeze; some obscure, but not the sun.

"I have eyed the bore of my own golden cord, like a sailor peering a spyglass. But I find no masts of distant ships and I find no distant shore. Instead, I see through gauzy veils, like the spray of salt on an outer lens. Yet my clouded view does not deny the knowing in my soul. For distant, lies the Face of God, and in spite of that brilliance all that is given to my sight are brightly glowing veils.

"Some I have learned to carefully part, others I have torn asunder, yet the light grows not in brightness but in finer grades of color.

"What do I see? Her veils! And yet not even most of these, for I can only recognize the gossamer I've come to know. And these are like acquaintances, each with a preference for delicate parting or merciless rending; each attuned to its own discord.

"And so I gaze and listen; I watch and I observe, cradling this question: 'What blocks the Face of God?' And when time has had its fill of me, I become like one lost in a cave and catching a mere glimpse of light, I gain a sense of where to go.

"For what is a charm but one sort of help? And what is help but one form of healing? And what is a healing but a parting of veils?"

THE TIDE

And I asked him, "Could a charm help my brother?" For he had run away when I was just six, off to find his fortune in a foreign land. For many years I grieved, as I did not know if he lived. I wondered if the spirit that overtook his soul ever gave him room enough to feel our common loss. And he answered me saying,

"Ah, Madeline!

"Pray for the tide, for the world is at work pulling us apart, like a ship caught in the winds of a violent sea. I am pulled to unite with my clan, I am pulled to unite with my mate; I am pulled to make my way in the world, I am pulled by the love in my heart; I am pulled to go and express myself, I am pulled by the world of ideas, and sometimes I am pulled by the Great One up above. Is it not a wonder that each of us is not found broken and sunk at the bottom of the sea?

"We enter as puppets or as clouds on the breeze. Yearning for spirit to flow through us and fill us with its pleasure. Seven winds are blowing, can we choose among them or are we as a boat without steerage, moving along by the waves and the wind?

"The tragedy is this—I believe I have a rudder and can choose the wind to blow me home. Even as the coast grows faint and the flocks of gulls grow thin to my stern, I set my jaw with certitude, for I am convinced of my skill as a sailor.

"Can anyone convince me that I sail to my doom? Look, I see a faint shoreline, and confidence swells me with pride. I shall die of exposure before I know it is a phantom. No help can reach me, not a charm or a kiss or a prayer, for I am owned by a seductive wind and my life is given to its whim.

"And yet, there is the tide. Mindless of the wind, careless of my sorry plight it breathes at me slowly. And in its gentleness I am stirred to quietude and find myself reflecting. Here amidst the swirling waters I am struck by a song in a higher key and awed by that chorus, I taste something new. Now I look back over the stern, now I see I have no rudder and wish inside for a new kind of wind. Not seven blowing aimlessly, but perhaps I can trim my sails so that two or three may blow as one, and so that I might carefully choose.

"Now there is hope for my sorry state. Now there is an opening for a task or a potion or even a charm. Your love for your brother is a golden cord that connects you both across time. Rest assured and pray, my dear, pray only for the tide."

INNER WISHES

Darkness came late in the summer and Simon worked till the last light. And he made me wonder at wishes, but mostly the wishes that clutched at my heart. He said an inner wish was rare. I asked him, "Why is this so?" And he answered saying,

"Ah, Madeline!

"An inner wish takes a strength uncommon in our time. A strength that grows by the thimble—full, yet drains away as easily as water runs through sand; lost to the cracks and fissures that bleed it out without value or sense."

And he was quiet for a long time, as if he was sleeping, but then he began again.

"Ah, Madeline!

"We enter this world and early on we are taught and learn so quickly. We learn to gain the attentions of those whose role it is to raise us. Is this easy? Is it hard? Do we struggle from day one with what should be freely given to the young? Or rather, is our struggle one of hiding for protection? In either case it amounts to the same discord, for as trees thin in the autumn without sap and without sun, so too does the soul wither if its hunt for trust is fruitless.

"But life tosses us all into a harsh and endless sea. So vast and so deep that one so afflicted will weaken in their cycles of turmoil and escape, never storing strength enough to form an inner wish. But will instead with selfish eyes and airs of high entitlement, acquire and collect to quench the parched thirst of their fears.

"And what of those among us who were made warm in the cold and given their fill of sustenance? What was their experience with the moods of their desires? Was that energy of play and exploration given sway? Was it nurtured to blossom and fruit into beauty or purpose or life? Or was it instead drained away like a channel poked in an earthen dam; that now breached the flow flows on without end? Or rather, was the lesson learned to conjure storms and fires? In either case it amounts to the same discord.

"But life tosses us all into a harsh and endless sea. So vast and so deep that one so afflicted will weaken in their cycles of creation and destruction, never storing strength enough to form an inner wish. But will thwart off any fortitude in the face of a worthy cause, instead seeking thrills yet finding betrayal.

"And what of those among us who were given space to fail until they could at last succeed? What was their sense of their place in the world? Did they find through their striving a way to bring value to those around them, and through this means satisfy themselves? Or was their inner sense corrupted, spoiled like grapes left to sour on the vine, leaving a hunger not filled by exchange and a thirst not quenched by the waters of fairness. Or rather was their lesson one of meekness in the face of strife? In either case it amounts to the same discord.

"But life tosses us all into a harsh and endless sea. So vast and so deep that one so afflicted will weaken in their cycles of tyranny and slavery, never storing strength enough to form an inner wish. But will instead dig with impropriety at the collections of all others, searching for leverage and always keeping score.

"And what of those who found treasure in serving those among us? Was the nest of their youth feathered with love? Did they learn to be patient with their own private yearnings? Or were these shown as trifles and to hide behind airs? Or rather was the lesson to be swept away in drama. In either case it amounts to the same discord. Like fish alive in a frozen pond, the heart lives below in the face of an icy coldness. Bottled up, it issues forth in fits of unforgiveness.

"But life tosses us all into a harsh and endless sea. So vast and so deep that one so afflicted will weaken in their cycles of unity and division, never storing strength enough to form an inner wish. But will instead always gush in love or hate or tears. Drowning in self-pity; never learning how to swim.

"And what of those among us who learned the fisherman's trick of untangling a net with the tools of the heart? Did they find a path to express their truths? Could they unite their own harmony with the greater songs around them? Or were they taught that truth was outside and breath meant just to recite other's words? Or rather was the lesson simply not to speak at all? In either case it amounts to the same discord. Like a castaway, alive without connection, the urge remains to find exchange. Though hope comes in floating a note in a bottle, insanity lurks in the unanswered call.

"But life tosses us all into a harsh and endless sea. So vast and so deep that one so afflicted will weaken in their cycles of expression and repression, never storing strength enough to form an inner wish. But will instead talk without end, cling without mercy and flee from abodes of silence and peace.

"And what of those among us who have found their song and learned to sing? Did they learn the art of reason as a ballast to their heart? Was 'thinking through' a talent worthy of attention? Or rather was the message one to leave that work alone, and sail through a lifetime only praying for safe crossing? Or rather, was the lesson one to live consumed by thought, and formulate and theorize without true understanding? In either case it amounts to the same discord. Starved or stuffed by reason the view is still the same, like a horse in blinders missing every lovely scene. Lost in foggy ignorance or chilled to the bone by icy sense, the mind shrivels before its time.

"But life tosses us all into a harsh and endless sea. So vast and so deep that one so afflicted will weaken in their cycles of conceit and of concede, never storing strength enough to form an inner wish. But will instead replay the past with fret and quick defense and live a life of arrogant and foolish speculation.

"And what of those among us for whom reason is a treasure? Who found the time and place in which to best explore this fortune? Were they given the experience while still open and still young of mystery and wonder at the life still new before them? Were they taught of their places below and above, and taught to remember the passing of life?

Or instead did they learn that there is no tomorrow, and the price on the bill never has to be paid? Or rather, did they learn to keep their feet as well as their heads in the clouds? In either case it amounts to the same discord. Like thieves in the night building mounds of treasure, without care of harm done or the chance to do good.

"But life tosses us all into a harsh and endless sea. So vast and so deep that one so afflicted will weaken in their cycles of doubt and of belief, never storing strength enough to form an inner wish. But will instead live large as if God answers just to him and in this ugly fantasy die lonely and insane."

He sighed a deep sigh, and took up his work. But I pressed him in a new way asking only this, "But people come to you for charms! They all must have an inner wish! They are not saints or sages, who have stored a lot of strength. The ones that I've seen are poor or sick. How can they cradle a firm inner wish?"

He put down his tool, and held an unfinished charm to the light, and gazed at the patterns that played all through it, turning it slow to the left and the right. And he placed it on his tabletop and he took a breath and said,

"Ah, Madeline!

"Those sheltered by their own discord are like contented sheep—fattened and slaughtered for their hides and their meat, never having hungered for an inner wish. But when ruin visits the wealthy, when sickness claims the robust, when loneliness strikes the famous or despair afflicts the proud! Then there is a crumbling and cracks form in the faults and there in the dust a crystal forms.

"It begins with the sense that my discord lives through me, yet I and it are not the same. Now I can see it as separate from me, even as it moves me, even as it drains me. Seeing this I store the strength to form an inner wish, a wish to find purpose or trust, a wish to see deeply or know how to serve, a wish to untangle knots deeply woven, or air what is true, or be tuned in to God. Now this wish burns like fire, warms like the sun and lights the way for something finer. That is when they come, knowing at last that they are not sheep."

He sighed again, but followed this with a deep inspiration; filling his chest and igniting his eyes and once again he worked on his carving.

THE MOON LAKE
WOMAN

And I asked him if one charm could help throughout the changes in a life. And he was silent for a moment and then he answered, saying, "Go east to Moon Lake. There you will meet a woman who, in the blossom of her youth, came to me with a wound in her heart. Her passions were like jasper, running hot and cooling quickly, each leaving a trace. Find her, and then ask her your question."

So I took the road to the mountains. Hidden amid the gentle peaks sat ancient Moon Lake, cold and clear. Sheltered from the winds, fed by mountain springs, it renews the spirits of those who come and drink its icy waters. Having no idea how to find the Moon Lake Woman, I lodged at an inn near the western shore, intent to rise early and watch the dawn play with the lake and the clouds and the mountains.

It was not quite spring, and the lake was empty of the throngs that flock to it in summer. The shore was deserted except for a bird, early for its season. The light of the morning lent first tones of gray to the mist and then ocher to the stones. Out in the lake were rocks polished smooth by the ages. Some large enough to row out to and sit upon. Others closer in were smaller; dry and pale above the water with dark, wet collars like painted on stripes. One of these had caught my eye. It wasn't striped like all the rest and its tones were more like silver than ocher. As I gazed upon it, it seemed to rise above the lake. And then I could see that it wasn't a rock, but the head of a silver-haired woman submerged, watching the dawn with her eyes level with the waters.

I was shocked to find I was not alone in the quiet of the morning. I was shocked to grasp that here was a person bearing the icy cold with a stillness of movement I could not comprehend. Perhaps the greatest shock was the sight of this old woman, like an apparition, emerging naked from the lake. Her skin was wrinkled, but her body was firm. She walked like a cat and silently sat beside me. I was dumbstruck, yet she paid no attention to my state. She gazed at me with eyes as still as the Moon Lake waters then turned her head to again watch the dawn.

My imagination was like a sword, cutting a path to vanity. Would I look like her when I reached her age? Could I carry myself with such elegant grace, exposing my deflated breasts and skin shriveled by a host of summers?

But soon she broke my reverie, "I used to watch the dawn from the shore but I'd get so lost in my own daydreams that I'd miss the ever changing colors. Now I gaze from in the lake and the cold, wet waters anchor me so that I cannot drift away."

She was covered in goosebumps yet she seemed content to simply let the morning sun warm and dry her skin. She dangled her calves in the water and signaled me to do the same. As soon as I did, my own cloud of dreams vanished like the morning mist.

"What brings you here?" she asked, and she turned to study my face. I looked at her for a moment and, collecting myself, I said, "My name is Madeline. I am learning from a man named Simon; he is a charm carver. I asked him a question about charms and he told me to find the Moon Lake Woman and bring to her my question."

A smile broke across her eyes and she breathed in deep at the trace of my words. She bowed her head and fingered the crimson stone that hung between her breasts. She asked, "What question has brought you to come all this way?"

And I looked into her eyes, and silently I got a kind of answer. But an answer I could not begin to formulate in words. So I asked the Moon Lake Woman, "How is it after a lifetime you rise and wear that charm? What outside of sentiment has kept it so dear through all of the changes in your life?"

The sun was cresting the trees, and the rays unfiltered by branches graced first our faces and shoulders, and then our elbows and knees until we were both fully in the sun. She passed her necklace over her head and down her silver hair. She handed it to me and asked, "What do you see?" I held the charm up close to my face. It was made from jasper, uniformly red. The jaspers I had seen were banded and swirly in layers of gray mixed with red. To find a piece of red this large would have taken patience and a fine sense of luck. The carving was simple. I said, "It is a monkey without ears holding up a peach, carved of a fine piece of jasper."

She lay flat on her back and closed her eyes and pointed her face towards the sun. She spoke to me slowly. "I was shy when I was young and my heart ached to be loved. My first love was a man from another land, here to find his riches. And I thought to myself that I was she, but to him I was just a warm companion while he was away from his home. I didn't believe he would leave, but my heart stirred like the sea before an approaching storm. One day my grandmother told me, "A charm carver has come to town. Go and have him carve you a charm." I thought that a charm might be just the thing to keep my love from leaving.

"Simon met me and I poured out my soul. He said that an unwilling heart could not be opened by a charm and yet, for any willing heart, a charm could help it open wider. I was convinced that my love really loved me and when my charm was ready I barely glanced at it and just put it on.

"In the face of the monkey I saw my love and the peach was his gift to me. A season passed and when I learned that my love was going to leave, I studied the charm and saw at last that the monkey had no ears. I cried, for I knew that my love would not listen to my pleas for him to stay. A year passed and I came to know that I had been his peach; in his hands only until he was done with me. And I grew cold towards even my memory of him. Two years passed and I came to know that I had been the monkey, clutching my love and not wanting to hear how our love was not meant to be. Three years passed and my peach was my heart, and I would not give it to any man for my ears had deceived me before. Seven years passed and my heart became soft and my peach became my sense that if I held the love of God in my hands, I would be content. Ten years past and I met my husband and my heart was full at last, and I thought of the monkey as a happy God, holding me, his happy peach. And even though my husband died many years ago, this charm remains a link to the path my heart has taken."

And she became silent.

The sun, now higher, warmed us. The Moon Lake Woman and I climbed higher on the shore. I asked her, "When you met Simon, did you talk to him about monkeys or peaches?" And she laughed and told me, "I spoke to him of none of those things. How he knew what to carve, what he sensed of the flow of my life . . . this I do not know. I only know that he is blessed and that he saw me with his heart."

DANCE

I remember a day near sunset watching Simon carve. His foot worked a pedal in steady rhythm that spun around a grinder. When jade touched the wheel it sang a song interrupted by dips in a water pot. The melody lulled away my thoughts and pulled me into the shape of the charm; an acorn I surmised, for a shy, gentle man who wished know what it was that was in him.

Simon worked into twilight, never asking for a lantern, and by degrees all shadows and highlights merged into a play on my eyes. The world appeared as if projected on a screen, yet a screen flawed by a texture and by an animation. The texture was like aged parchment or like a pumice stone, and the animation was a kind of shimmering. The effect gave life to the room and life to the workbench and Simon and the jade shared a faint glow.

As he carved the cup of the acorn, a change came over the room. The song of the jade pitched higher, the rhythm of his pedal grew, and the shimmering began to swirl. With this I felt a knot and a pang and sensed a flood of panic. At once, the cup broke in a high-pitched *tik!* and Simon's working came to a halt. I sat in silence, no longer anxious, and finally ventured to ask, "What will you do now that the acorn's broke?" And he answered, saying,

"Ah, Madeline!

"I once saw a horse in a pasture and watched her calmly grazing. She ruminated slowly, and as she gazed at me I thought if I moved slow as well that I could mount and ride her. Slow did I approach, and she was not troubled. Slow did I stroke her, and she was most agreeable. I planned in my mind just how I would mount, and when I was certain, I leapt, yet to my shock, she quickly kicked me in the teeth! The world, you see, is not as it seems. And so we are obliged to dance!

"Twilight descends, and we appear nearer to what we are. The brightness of the day obscures the softer light of spirit-snow. Tonight you saw her outer veils, but guard your heart from racing, resist the hunger of your mind. For what you see is like the horse, enchanting yet without mercy.

"How lovely are the swirls of jade, like frozen spirit-snow. Born of a dance in an underground cauldron, is it any wonder how graceful it endures? Or why it always lends a charm a flavor of eternity?

74

"Yet jade cannot forever endure, for can I not cut it with dust on a string? Born in one dance, it dies in another. Is it not the same with us?

"In the wink of a blink in the eye of this jade, I shall be just dust, my traces blowing in these fields, perhaps to turn to stone again in seven million years? And yet perhaps three traces will endure. My charms and what I've placed in them; you my dear, with my love in your heart; and if I am blessed, my soul will emerge from this, my own cauldron-dance, enduring like the jade.

"Now the spirit-snow dances, like a fog about to unveil. Shall I surmise what mystery I'm about to see; and drain away the magic, and sterilize the sacredness? For my imagination is like a sharpened sword—it cuts the fog and fills me with a certainty even if I am wrong. Even though I've seen my way to hop astride that horse, in the moment of that seeing, I am no more than blind, and the world is quick to cause me to stumble.

"Better that we learn to dance, better that we apportion our surmise like a miser counting coins, better that we read our waves then drown within our passions. And dance with the spirit-snow; follow with a stillness and a wish to see. And you, my dear, will gain a sense of your own enduring grace.

"The spirit-snow fades in the light of the morning, and then I shall lead in the dance of this charm. But never was it an acorn, but an acorn without and a bell from within. Tomorrow I shall carve the clapper that I've just begun. Dance, my dear—life is just dance, yet if we can only see, yet if we can only sense when to follow and when to lead!"

THE SEAMSTRESS

One day a seamstress came around, looking for a charm. She was old and hunched with gnarled, angled fingers and a face all squinty from years of close work. And sighs filled up her silences and her palms gestured up towards the sky. "I've spent my life working pieces" she said, "patching knees and sewing hems. But never a dress of my own design, for many are those who seek a patch and rare the one who wants something new. For I have seen my life in the bottom of my sewing bag and fear I'll be remembered only as a mender."

Simon asked for her bag and emptied it onto his bench. It was filled with scraps of cloth and tiny bits of thread, a treasure for a bird or mouse from which to make a nest. To me it looked chaotic with no thread connecting all the things. Simon looked at the pile, then looked at the woman and said, "Return to me tomorrow, and you shall have your charm." And the seamstress left with a notable sigh.

And I marveled as Simon looked through his stones, settling at last on a rough piece of jade. And I asked him, "What will you carve for the seamstress?" And as he worked, he answered, saying,

"Ah, Madeline!

"Vultures and maggots are both the same, eating only the flesh of the dead. And yet we are repulsed by these, but they are just as janitors, cleaning up the waste. For we are flesh and tasty for a thousand kinds of things, all eager to devour and reduce us back to dust. And yet there is another thing that beckons sweet and savory—morsels delightful for a different sort of scavenger. Without death and rot, indeed without dying we offer up a banquet serving scraps of our attention.

"How willingly we cut and chop and dice up our attention. Making it digestible to those who have no teeth! For solid and whole, attention is not savory, and thus it can grow in toughness and strength. But we are compelled by life itself to offer up this sacrifice, compelled by feelings that start with 'I should.' But, thanks be to God for we may resist this pull as strong as gravity. For buried deep burns the flame of conscience; that knitter of our pieces, that weaver of our remnants, that fuser of our elements; forging an essence tougher than jade.

"And yet we are each a poor lighthouse keeper, enchanted by the sound of the rain, we forget to fuel the beacon. And by degrees the lamp grows dim, till ships can't plot a proper course. And we cry and mourn as the ships go down, and wring our hands at the furious sea, because we've forgotten not only the lamp but even the long stairway up, and even where the doorway lies.

"But even the enchanted know that life will end. And then the lighthouse keeper finds he's captain of a ship—out in the rain, searching for the beacon, sober to his likely fate.

"And sober now, the spell is gone, and even near the end, the knitting and the weaving always reignite the flame."

And he worked at his bench well into that night, and when he was done he placed the charm, finished, into the cup my hands. It was shaped like a circle, without source or ending. And though it was carved from solid jade, he textured it like woven cloth. And the weaving of the cloth seemed to echo gnarled fingers. And the jade he chose had colors of green and brown and violet and pale. And he worked these into the carving like different colored threads, looking as if they had come from the bottom of a sewing bag and then had turned to stone.

The seamstress came the next morning and when she saw her charm, she kissed Simon's hands and cried without ceasing.

THE CHIMNEY

Simon ended his work each day in a most peculiar way. His shop was warmed by an open hearth that he fed with logs in the morning. By late in the day the room was warmed by all the rocks that he placed by the flames. But he never stoked the fire in the afternoon, and the hearth became cool by the end of the day. After he had carved his last he rose from his bench and went to the hearth. Armed with a brush, a rasp and a file he swept the chimney then hoisted up and took to honing the walls. I'd hear him shimmy to the top and hear the rasp and filings. He'd work his way down and stop and polish any flaw in the chimney wall. And then he'd emerge all sooty, saying, "What a fine day of work this was," and then we would part till the morning.

And this made me wonder. And I asked him, "Why each night do you clean the chimney? Do seven logs leave such a trace? And why each night do you hone the walls—after all, the soot cannot pit them?" And he answered saying,

"Ah, Madeline!

"Each night I wish for peaceful sleep, but never would it come, if I did not polish the bore of my chimney. For in its nooks and crannies lie the problems of the day, each an obstruction to passing breezes, each a maker of whirlpools and eddies, each a kind of hindrance that burdens every gentle flow.

"And I pray for a gentle spirit to animate my limbs and cause me to carve beyond my skill. And I pray for a kindly spirit to overtake my heart and drive me to compassion beyond my poor capacity. And I pray for a wizened spirit to whisper in my ear perhaps more truth than I can bear. And who am I that gentle wisps would struggle down to reach, fighting every rampart that I have left behind?

"How easily I grow content and settle back all satisfied! How simple simply to allow all common airs through me. But here there is an awful cost, for then I give my life to them and what then is my earned reward—devouring eyes, a flinty heart and an endless need for stroking.

"The greatest of the burdens lies in chimneys filled with soot. Then just the coarsest of winds can blow through. And I am left unchangeable—set in my tempo, set in my ways, without any chance to hear or see newness. Then I am like a common stone unchangeable except into dust.

"Perhaps to you its wasted force to climb and scrub and polish, and yet I say that nothing else so fills me up with life. Men and women mark their days heaving their burdens way up a mountain, all too often falling short for want of extra force.

"Is there a path to store it up? I say it is simple—find your chimney and scrub out the flaws, polish it with reverence! And fashion it to welcome in the finest of the heavens. Then the burdens lighten, the mountain seems a hill, and though my muscles heave all day I suffer no exhaustion. For though I am sooty, I am renewed, and filled with my wishes, I rest, content."

HELP

One morning at the shore, the wind was steady from the north. Its boldness chilled my face and toes and slowly dread consumed me. Winter beckoned and the sea would turn both treacherous and cold. And I knew that Simon's boat would not stand the heavy winds. And soon, my bones told me, he'd need to depart.

I was not pining but filled with dread at the thought of my coming confession. From him I had learned what blocked people's striving and what could open their way. And though he had taught me about stones and carving, I knew that my knack would never be charms.

And I cursed the weakness of my will and I cursed my lack of talent. Despite all his teaching, his shoes were not for me to fill. And I would have to tell him this and I would disappoint him. And knowing this I found that I was torturing my heart.

For days I hid myself from him, but filled to overflowing now, I burst into his shop and found him polishing intently. The sight of him calmed me; the pace of his working steadied my soul. He held me gently in his gaze, seeing every facet and flaw, as if I were a precious stone that held his admiration. In silence, he resumed, yielding me space to locate my words.

In a flood, I confessed. I told him I was grateful, and that I'd always love him, and though I wished to please him I could never master charms. And so, I said, "I'm sorry." And quiet overtook us both. And finally he spoke, saying,

"Ah, Madeline!

"When I was small I saw a girl cry at a kiss from an ugly boy. His kiss was like a shackle being added to her chain. Later on I broke my arm and a kiss stopped me from crying. A kiss can be a thousand things and some of them are helpful. And I have learned a few of these, but never could I master every kind of kiss.

"And years ago our king was killed by an evil potion. Yet I have been at deathbeds, and seen the moribund revived, with finely crafted potions, made from sacred flowers. Potions can be many things and some of them are helpful. And I have learned a few of these, but never could I master every kind of potion.

"And when I was a quarryman, mining blocks of stone, my foreman enslaved us with hard, heartless tasks. Yet some of these lifted the ignorance from me. A task can be a thousand things and some of these are helpful. And I have learned a few of these, but never could I master every kind of task.

"And I have looked for answers, and some cost me dearly when they weren't true. Yet others, like the sun above, illuminate my days. Answers can be many things and some of them are helpful. And I have learned a few, but never could I master every kind of answer.

"And questions still fill me. And I have held questions that torment my soul and I have held others that light the unknown. They can be so many things and some of them are helpful. And I have learned a few of these, but never could I master every kind of question.

"And I have seen blessings that bind souls to idols, while others align them with the Divine. Blessings can be many things and some of them are helpful. And I have learned a few of these, but never could I master every kind of blessing.

"But charms for me are different. Carved with bad intentions they are like millstones, weighing one down even to hell. Yet carved with good intentions, and clarity and light, they illuminate the link that binds a soul to heaven. A charm is but a wish, confined, but to be of any help, the wish must be weighed, the stone must be known, the carving, precise; the polishing, perfect. And I have only shown you precious few of these."

And his hands continued polishing even as he spoke. But when he fell silent, his hands became still; his work, at last finished. And he threaded the charm on a necklace of silk to hang above a heart. And he held it up to the morning light and turned it left and then to the right. The stone was flawless amethyst, carved as a tiny sword, the handle darkly purple, the blade just faintly pale. And, satisfied, he blew his breath upon it, and looking deeply in my eyes, he handed it to me.

"Ah, Madeline!

"I knew from the first that carving charms would never be your path. And yet I am contented, for you have learned so much. I know a path will find you, touching your passion and touching your mind, and you'll learn to master that which you'll do. My heartfelt pride is not in that, but only is in this—in what you do I know that you will absolutely be."

And he kissed me on the forehead as I gazed upon my charm. And he left the shop for what I thought was just a morning stroll. I didn't see his shop was bare and by the time I noticed, he was rowing out to sea. I put on my charm and I ran to the shore and shouted out his name, but the north wind was blowing and it swallowed my screams. And I listened for his voice amidst the crashing of the breakers. But he was then beyond the waves and straining to hear, my ears were no help. And yet I heard his voice emerge from just beneath my charm.

"Ah, Madeline!" I felt him say, "Your heart is now secure."

GAZING OUT

And now the sun sets to the south; the days are cold, and I find myself yearning. Not for the warmth of another summer, and not for the thrill of a still distant shore; for I have lost my taste for these. I yearn for what will come tomorrow, knowing I am ready.

My vessel will be empty soon and melt into the ground. I've heard that our bones make the grasses grow strong, and I rest contentedly in this, that I will help the grasses.

My love will live a little longer, held in the hearts of those I've embraced. And I rest contentedly in this, that love survives the Great Divide.

But of all I learned from Simon, it now comes down to this—what will become of the fruits of my work? "Only a third," he told me one day, "will any person ever see." And I asked him about this, and he answered, saying,

"Ah, Madeline!

"Long have you watched me carving at stones, but close as you watch, you can perceive just a third of my fruits. For effort always splits in threes, one part sits here on the bench, one part rises up to heaven, yet the last contains the chance to live on out beyond our days.

"For we are but as vessels filled with just an outbreath of heaven. But heaven must as well inhale and soon the spirit, briefly ours, must return from whence it came. From this we gain the spark of life and heaven gains a spirit now that's filled with newer flavors. And when my life is over any spirit that remains is like a drop of ocean spray returning to the sea. For spirit is an ocean, and we are not the fish, but drops to mix and mingle; dissolved and uncontained.

"And yet if I collect myself—my body focused on my task, my mind in quiet openness, my heart preparing to receive—then the forces that forge all the gems; the rubies and the diamonds, the emeralds and the pearls; work to form a gem in me—a soul that can endure.

"But if I work halfhearted, or partially distracted, or carve a form in carelessness then nothing will be crystallized. Instead my precious third just merely dissipates as heat, warming up a chilly world from which I'll fade without a trace.

"For we can forge a heavenly gem—never to melt in the endless ocean; forever to endure, forever to remain."

Now I sit as the sun goes down, my breath returning to the sea. But I am content with the gem in my heart and thankful for Simon who showed me. Now I sit as the sun goes down and winter calls my name.

To order more copies of

THE CHARM CARVER

or for information about bulk ordering for reading
groups or for the retail trade,
please call 1-800 431-1579,
or go to www.thecharmcarver.com